LET'S-READ-AND-FIND-OUT SCIENCE®

STAGE **1**

My Five Senses

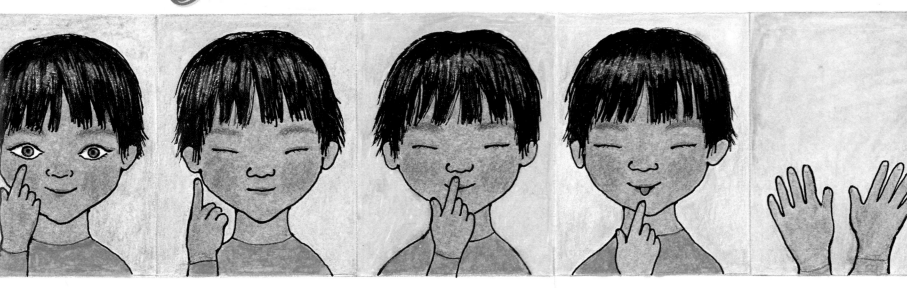

by Aliki

HarperCollins Publishers

for my sister, Helen Lambros

The *Let's-Read-and-Find-Out Science* book series was originated by Dr. Franklyn M. Branley, Astronomer Emeritus and former Chairman of the American Museum–Hayden Planetarium, and was formerly co-edited by him and Dr. Roma Gans, Professor Emeritus of Childhood Education, Teachers College, Columbia University. Text and illustrations for each of the books in the series are checked for accuracy by an expert in the relevant field. For more information about Let's-Read-and-Find-Out Science books, write to HarperCollins Children's Books, 10 East 53rd Street, New York, NY 10022 or visit our web site at http://www.harperchildrens.com.

HarperCollins®, ▰®, and Let's Read-and-Find-Out Science® are trademarks of HarperCollins Publishers Inc.

MY FIVE SENSES
Copyright © 1962, 1989 by Aliki Brandenberg
Manufactured in China.
For information address HarperCollins Children's Books, a division of HarperCollins Publishers, 10 East 53rd Street, New York, NY 10022.

Library of Congress Cataloging-in-Publication Data
Aliki.
  My five senses.
  (Let's-read-and-find-out science. Stage 1)
  Summary: A simple presentation of the five senses, demonstrating some ways we use them.
  ISBN 0-690-04792-4. — ISBN 0-690-04794-0 (lib. bdg.). — ISBN 0-06-445083-X (pbk.)
  1. Senses and sensation—Juvenile literature. [1. Senses and sensation.] I. Title. II. Series.
QP434.A43 1989   88-35350
612'.8

Revised Edition

My Five Senses

I see	I hear	I taste	I smell	I touch

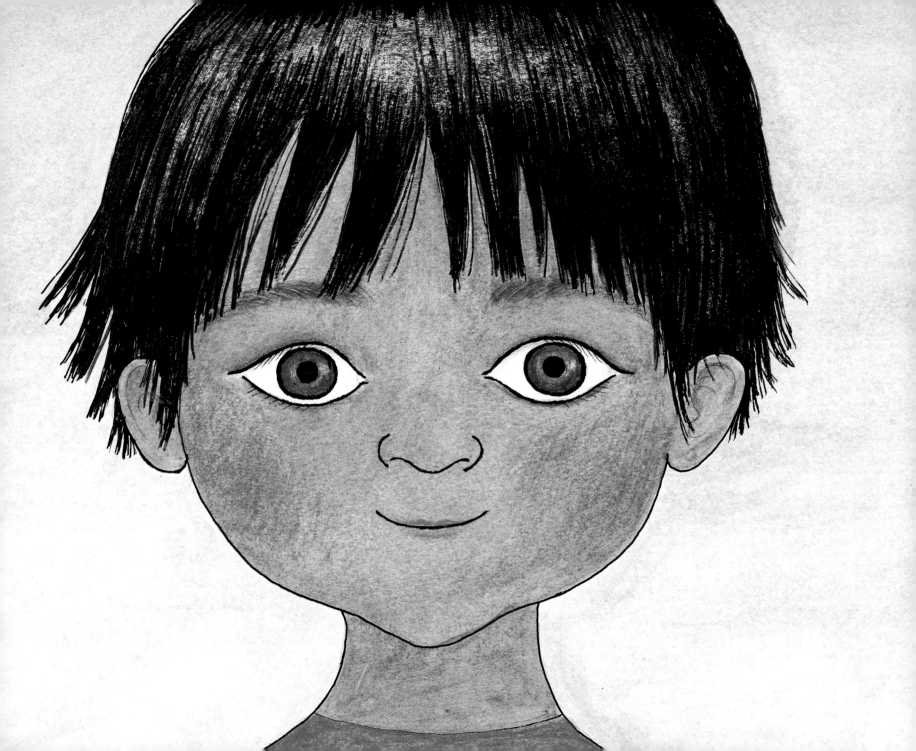

I can see! I see with my eyes.

I can hear! I hear with my ears.

I can smell! I smell with my nose.

I can taste! I taste with my tongue.

11

I can touch! I touch with my fingers.

I do all this with my senses.
I have five senses.

When I see the sun or a frog

or my baby sister,

I use my sense of sight. I am seeing.

When I hear a drum or a fire engine

or a bird,

I use my sense of hearing.

I am hearing.

Cuando huelo el jabón, un pino
o galletas recién horneadas,
uso el sentido del olfato:
Huelo.

Cuando bebo leche o como,
uso el sentido del gusto:
Saboreo.

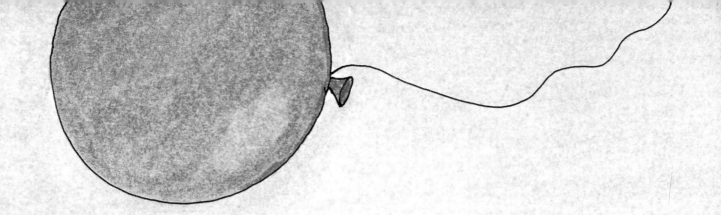

Cuando toco un gatito, un globo o el agua,

uso el sentido del tacto:

Toco.

Algunas veces, uso todos los sentidos al mismo tiempo.

Otras, uso sólo uno.

Me encanta jugar a adivinar qué sentidos uso.

Cuando miro la luna y las estrellas,

uso un solo sentido:

el de la vista.

Cuando río y juego con mi perrito,
uso cuatro sentidos:
la vista, el oído, el olfato y el tacto.

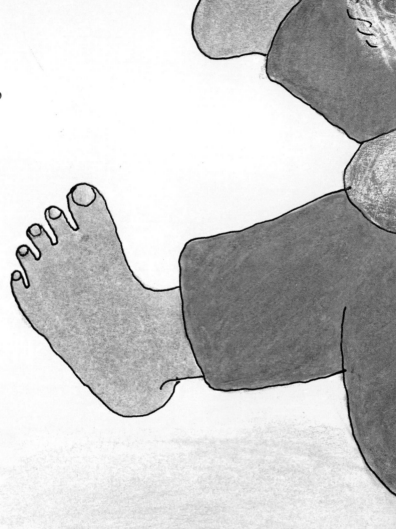

Cuando hago que la pelota rebote, uso tres sentidos:
la vista, el oído y el tacto.

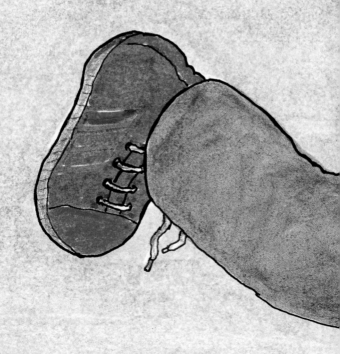

A veces, uso un sentido más que otro.
Pero todos ellos son muy importantes
porque gracias a los cinco sentidos
me doy cuenta de lo que ocurre a mi alrededor.

Darse cuenta de lo que nos rodea es ver todo lo que hay que ver . . .

oír todo lo que hay que oír . . .

oler todo lo que hay que oler . . .

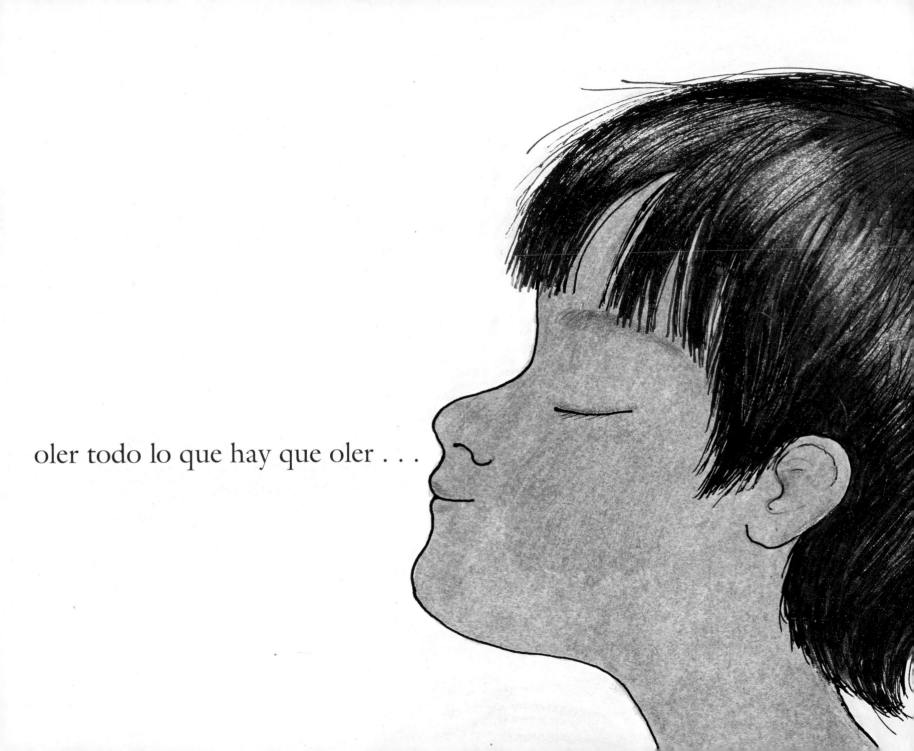

saborear todo lo que hay que saborear . . .

tocar todo lo que hay que tocar.

Mis sentidos trabajan
cada minuto del día.
No importa a dónde vaya
o lo que haga.

Gracias a ellos, me doy cuenta
de lo que pasa a mi alrededor.